Get Off The Tablet

Written by Olivia Griffin & Nadia Griffin   Illustrated by Uliana Barabash

"Ask your mommy or daddy to help you make this delicious tropical drink. Have fun!"

That sounds good, Nadia thought to herself about the drink video that she just watched on her tablet.

Nadia walked towards the kitchen with her tablet and the taste of tropical goodness.

"Mommy, I want to make a tropical drink!" said Nadia.

"GET OFF THE TABLET!" said Nadia' mommy. "What can I do?" Nadia asked "I'm bored!"

"If you are bored you can always read a book, play with your toys, or go over flashcards." said Nadia's mommy.

"I will just go back on my tablet," Nadia whispered as she continued to watch videos on her tablet.

"Hey guys, welcome to my video. Let's do the slime challenge!"

"Olivia let's do this slime chall-," Nadia said before being cut off by her sister.
"Didn't mommy tell you to GET OFF THE TABLET? "asked Olivia.
"I'm going to tell mommy, "yelled Olivia.
"No, I'll get off the tablet!" replied Nadia.

As Nadia walked out of the room, she decided to go back downstairs with her tablet.

"Nadia, I'm going to the store. Do you want to come with me?" Nadia's daddy asked.

"I can get that unicorn toy I saw on the unboxing video," Nadia whispered.

"YES, I want to go to the store!" Nadia replied as she ran towards the door to leave with her daddy.

"Daddy, can we go by the toys?" asked Nadia.

"Why do you want to go by the toys?" asked Nadia's daddy.

"I want to get a unicorn toy," replied Nadia.

"You already have a lot of toys," said Nadia's daddy.

As Nadia was asking for a unicorn toy, her daddy noticed she was watching a video on her tablet of a unicorn toy.
"GET OFF THE TABLET!" said Nadia's daddy.

Nadia's mommy and sister were in the garage when Nadia and her daddy came back home.

"We are about to go on a bike ride. Do you two want to join us?" Nadia's mommy asked.

Daddy thought about Nadia being on the tablet and how going on a bike ride as a family could help Nadia stay off the tablet.

"Yes, we all should go for a bike ride," Nadia's daddy answered.
"Ok, put on your helmets and let's go," Nadia's mommy replied.

Nadia's sister looked at her riding her bike, smiling and having fun. "Are you bored now?" Nadia's sister asked.

"No, I'm having so much fun!" Nadia answered. "Can't say GET OFF THE TABLET to me!

They all laughed.

"Sometimes you need to get off your device and enjoy life"

-Olivia Griffin & Nadia Griffin

No part of this publication may be reproduced, stored in a retrieval system, or transmitted in any form or by any means, electronic, mechanical, photocopying, recording, or otherwise, without written permission of the publisher.

ISBN 978-1-7369393-0-7

Text copyright© 2021 by Bookfly Publishing.
Illustrations copyright© 2021 by Uliana Barabash.
All rights reserved. Published by Bookfly Publishing
www.bookflypublishing.com

Printed in the U.S.A.

CPSIA information can be obtained
at www.ICGtesting.com
Printed in the USA
LVHW070906180521
687738LV00001B/4